CHALLENGE YOUR KIDS

100 ENGAGING PROBLEMS AND RIDDLES FOR TEACHERS AND PARENTS TO USE

VOLUME 1

DAVE VACCARO

DEDICATION

This book is dedicated to all the teachers and parents who challenge their kids to solve problems in school and at home. I hope this book helps you reach your kids and support their growth.

ACKNOWLEDGMENTS

I wish to acknowledge my wife Leslie who has supported my writing efforts through her sound advice, encouragement and insight. She has been patient with me during the many hours of preparing this manuscript as well as the launching of this book. Thank you, Leslie.

My son Stephen Vaccaro and his wife Firouzeh have given me supportive comments and good advice in preceding forward with this writing project. I am thankful for their input and assistance.

Rita Toews designed this book cover and I am grateful for her time and her design work. She showed a great deal of patience as we went through the book cover design process.

I want to thank Lisa Hope, a teacher of gifted students, and her elementary school students for allowing me to present these problems and for giving me meaningful feedback.

Finally, I wish to express my gratitude to my daughter Stephanie Vaccaro. She has spent tireless hours editing this book as well as promoting this book. In addition, Stephanie has developed our website. Without Stephanie's work and input, this book could not have been completed or published. She has been the driving force in the development of *CHALLENGE YOUR KIDS.* Thank you Stephanie for all of your excellent work on this writing project. You are awesome.

Table of Contents

INTRODUCTION

Given the complexities of the world today, the ability to solve difficult problems is becoming increasingly more valuable. Much of our success as individuals, as well as communities, depends on the capacity to solve problems. Building this capacity in children—to consider relevant information, to reflect, and to analyze—helps to prepare them for the challenges that lie ahead.

This book provides 100 opportunities for kids to think through problems in an enjoyable way. It is intended to be used by teachers and parents with groups of children, as few as two or three or as many as thirty. It is not designed as a solo endeavor. A group setting allows them to develop the capacity to work together and to think critically, while finding the correct solution.

Although the problems may have multiple answers due to the open nature some of them possess, it is my intent to have your children burrow down to the one correct answer that I have provided. The process of digging down is the important work to help your kids develop the capacity to think. Almost all of these problems are based on real life. While a few are theoretical, they are still worthy of consideration. The journey of figuring out the answer is much more important than the actual answer itself because it builds both an awareness of their own abilities as well as the value of solving problems with others, a process no doubt they will repeat many times in life.

HOW TO USE THIS BOOK EFFECTIVELY

I have used each of these problems with students in elementary and middle school classrooms. I have also used these problems at home with my own children, nieces, nephews, and grandchildren. Virtually every time I have had great success, and the children say, "Give us another problem!" Even now, years later, my grand-nieces and grand-nephews ask me for one of my problems every time they see me.

The book is organized into three levels: beginning, intermediate, and advanced. These labels are an approximation because what may be easy for one kid may be difficult for another. You will have to decide what is appropriate for your kids.

To have the greatest impact, below are recommendations of how best to present these problems.

1. With few exceptions, I read the problems <u>aloud</u> to the kids, which helps develop their auditory abilities. Often, I will reread it.

2. I allow them to make guesses as I call on them, with a few exceptions. The problems where I request that they write their answers down and not share them include: "Line and Circles," "Codes," and "Squares." I'll walk around and check their answers, giving my usual feedback and asking them not to share their answers. This approach gets more mileage out of the problem and more attempts from everyone present.

3. Encouragement is important. When a guess is incorrect but reasonable, I may say that the guess is good, but it is not the correct one. Or, I may tell them that is an excellent answer, but unfortunately it is not the correct one; that it is a great answer but not the right one; or that it is very interesting, but we are not there yet. Positive feedback helps to encourage them to keep at it until they solve the problem.

4. I try to avoid using the hint. However, when necessary and to avoid frustration, you may wish to give them the hint. Each problem has a hint and an answer listed in the back of the book.

5. I <u>never</u> tell them the answer. Doing so undermines the whole process. This may drive the kids a bit crazy, but it enhances the sense of accomplishment when they finally solve it and shows them that they are capable of solving difficult problems.

6. When they do get the correct answer I'll brag on them, and I usually give them a quarter or some small token. Giving quarters is not required, but it does motivate them to tackle the next problem, and it recognizes their successes. It also makes it fun.

7. Another method is to allow yes or no answer questions to help them pare down the options. This is useful for digging down to the correct answer.

8. Do not allow your students or kids to use the internet to find the solution <u>during</u> the session. The solution must come from their own minds.

9. If the session ends before they solve the problem, they likely will try to solve it using the internet at home. However, I encourage them <u>not</u> to do this. I prefer that they think through the problems. This is where the real value can be derived.

10. The problems can be used in a variety of ways in the classroom. A problem could be used as a hook at the beginning of a lesson, as transitional tool between learning activities, or as a way to close a lesson.

100 Engaging Problems and Riddles for Teachers and Parents to Use

Chapter One

BEGINNING PROBLEMS

1. Tennis Tournament

In a regional tennis tournament, the eventual champion will be determined from 128 competitors by single elimination. When one of the competitors loses a match, he is eliminated from further play.

Question:

How many matches are played in order to arrive at the eventual champion?

Hint and Answer on page 41

2. River Rocks

A man had landscape workers put down 60 linear feet of river rock, including a felt bottom, to strengthen a small drainage ditch. They did a good job. After several weeks went by, he checked on the drainage ditch, and it appeared that someone moved about 10 feet of rock downstream leaving a bare spot. He put the rocks back in their original position, removing the bare spot. Three weeks later it happened again, leaving still another bare spot.

Question:

Can you explain how this happened?

Hint and Answer on page 41

3. Ant Survival

Fire ants are quite resilient. They are native to Brazil, but they have made their way to the United States by ships and other carriers. They have been known to survive several natural catastrophes, one of which is flooding.

Question:
How do fire ants manage to survive flooding?

Hint and Answer on page 42

4. Millie

Millie fell asleep at work, and no one knew about it. Even though her boss and some of her fellow workers had walked past her desk, no one realized what was happening.

Question:
How was this possible?

Hint and Answer on page 42

5. The Tortoise

The sulcata tortoise can live up to 100 years or more and weigh as much as 225 lbs. It is one of the largest tortoises in the world. A large one fell over onto its back in his enclosure at the Taipei Zoo in Taiwan. This was not good news for a tortoise.[1]

Question:
How did he get upright again?

Hint and Answer on page 42

6. The Bus Driver

In the state of Washington, you become the driver of a 65-passenger bus that can travel at 45 miles per hour or a 45-passenger bus that can travel 65 miles per hour.

Question:
How old is the driver?

Hint and Answer on page 43

7. Two Coins

I have two coins in my pocket that total 55 cents. Keep in mind that one of the coins is not a nickel.

Question:
What are the two coins?

Hint and Answer on page 43

8. The Same Bass

Jim went bass fishing on a nearby lake. At first he caught a few small pan fish but no bass. Then suddenly he got the strike he was hoping for, and he caught a nice 3 lb. bass. It was a good fight, and the bass made one jump out of the water. Finally, the man landed the fish. In the end, he released the bass back into the lake. The next day he caught the same bass.

Question:
How did he know it was the same bass?

Hint and Answer on page 43

9. Where to Build

There are many places where people can build houses and many types of building materials that can be used for construction.

Question:
Where can you build a house so that all four sides face south?

Hint and Answer on page 44

10. How Many?

The Ark was built to save mankind from the great flood. It was an enormous undertaking, and it took a very long time to construct. When it was finally finished the animals were herded onto the Ark.

Question:
How many animals of each kind did Moses have on the Ark?

Hint and Answer on page 44

11. The Election

Leslie ran for political office. She had many more votes than her opponent, yet she did not win the election.

Question:
How could this have happened?

Hint and Answer on page 44

12. Finding Values

$O + O = 18$
$X + X + X = 18$
$O + X + Y = 18$

Question:
What are the values of O, X, and Y?

Hint and Answer on page 45

13. The Big Hawaiian

There were two Hawaiians standing on a corner. One was a big Hawaiian and the other was a little Hawaiian. The little Hawaiian was the son of the big Hawaiian, but the big Hawaiian was not the father of the little Hawaiian.

Question:
Who was the big Hawaiian?

Hint and Answer on page 45

14. The Elevator

A woman lives on the 12th floor of her apartment building. Every morning she gets on the elevator and rides to the first floor and then off to work she goes. Every evening when she returns from work, she rides the elevator to the 9th floor and walks up the remaining three flights of stairs.

Question:
Why does she do this each day?

Hint and Answer on page 45

15. Blue Hen Chicken

I am the first state to ratify the U.S. Constitution. About 500 descendants of the Nanticoke Tribe still live within my borders. The Blue Hen Chicken is our official state bird.

Question:
Which state am I?

Hint and Answer on page 46

16. You Know Me

I never wear gloves, though I have hands. I never wear a mask, though I do have a face. I never wear earmuffs or a scarf when it is cold.

Question:
Who am I?

Hint and Answer on page 46

17. Christmas

People there just wanted to go swimming or sip on cold drinks in the shade, but it was Christmas Day, December 25. The weather was in the high 80s and incredibly warm. A visitor thought to himself, so this is Christmas.

Question:
Can you explain this occurrence?

Hint and Answer on page 46

18. Spooky

The man hated driving down a lonely, spooky road through woods that were rumored to be haunted. It gave him the creeps. The hair on the back of his neck stood up. The trip was five grueling miles long, and the lights on his car were not working.

Question:
How was he able to drive home safely?

Hint and Answer on page 47

19. Quicksand

Marie went hiking along the British Coast. After an hour had passed, she accidently stepped into a quicksand pit. She started to sink down to her waist, but she was sure that she would get out safely. However, the quicksand was not her biggest problem.[2]

Question:
What problem was worse than being trapped in the quicksand?

Hint and Answer on page 47

20. Innocent

Many years ago, a man was convicted of a bank robbery. Seven eyewitnesses testified that he was the bank robber. He claimed that he didn't do it, and he didn't know who did. He was sentenced to twenty years in prison for a crime he did not commit. After he served ten years of his sentence, he was freed and the real robber was sent to prison.

Question:
Can you explain how this outcome might occur?

Hint and Answer on page 47

Chapter Two

INTERMEDIATE PROBLEMS

21. The Paddle

One day, a man and his son Stephen went fishing. At the end of the day as they were loading the boat onto the trailer, his son dropped a paddle into the water. The paddle was carried slowly away from the shore.

Question:
How did they get the paddle back without putting the boat back into the water again?

Hint and Answer on page 49

22. Mary

Mary was not considered a beauty, and some would say that she was ordinary. On the other hand, Tom was what you might call a lady-killer and very handsome. Here is the problem. Mary is lying on the floor, and she is dead. Tom is standing over her body. There is broken glass and water on the floor.

Question:
How did Mary die?

Hint and Answer on page 49

23. Safe Crossing

A man needs to cross a river in a rowboat. With him, he has a chicken, a fox, and a bag of feed. He can only take one of these across the river at a time.

Question:
In what order can he successfully take these three across the river in the boat without the chicken eating the feed or the fox eating the chicken?

Hint and Answer on page 50

24. Two Buckets

You have a five-gallon bucket, a three-gallon bucket, and a water hose. The problem is that you only need four gallons of water.

Question:
Using just these two buckets and the water hose, how can you get the four gallons of water that you need?

Hint and Answer on page 50

25. Squares

Look at the figure below.

Question:

How many squares are in this figure? <u>Write</u> down your answer and do not share it with anyone else.

Hint and Answer on page 51

26. Candy Limit

I am a state where it is forbidden for one citizen to give another a box of candy that weighs more than 50 lbs. My original economy was developed around gold mining. Hell's Canyon, located here, is the deepest gorge in the United States.

Question:
Which state am I?

Hint and Answer on page 51

27. Line and Circles

<u>Draw</u> the figure below and do not share your answer with anyone else.
- Without crossing over a line
- Without backtracking
- Without taking your pencil off the paper

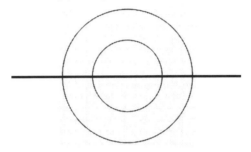

Hint and Answer on page 52

28. Four Things

I have been alone on this tree-lined and vegetated island since our plane crashed. Unfortunately, there were no other survivors. Within hours, I had given up the idea that anyone would rescue me anytime soon. I knew there were four things that I must do immediately to survive.

Question:
What are the four most important things that I need to do in order to survive? In what order should these be done?

Hint and Answer on page 52

29. Still Standing

One Virginia man has experienced something quite unusual. According to some experts, this natural event only occurs to one out of every 1,000,000 people. However depending on which of the fifty states you live in, this number can be higher or lower. Nonetheless, it has happened to him seven times.[3]

Question:
What is this event?

Hint and Answer on page 53

30. The Fall

In New York City, Sam fell off the Empire State Building, which is 102 stories high or 1250 feet, not counting its antenna spiral. Amazingly, he survived without injury. When Sam landed he simply walked away.

Question:
How was this possible?

Hint and Answer on page 53

31. Coded Message

Coded messages have been used for centuries. In wartime, spies have used these coded messages to avoid capture and detection. You can use coded messages to keep your own ideas private from outside detection.

Question:
Can you decode the following message? <u>Write</u> down your answer and do not share it with anyone else.
Message: 20-15 / 5-18-18 / 9-19 / 8-21-13-1-14 /
20-15 / 6-15-18-7-9-22-5 / 9-19 / 4-9-22-9-14-5

Hint and Answer on page 54

32. The Pool

The young boy disliked taking swimming lessons in the summers. It didn't seem like any fun, and his eyes burned when swimming in the pool. However, he did float well in the water. His friends in other cities had more pleasant experiences while taking swimming lessons.

Question:
What caused him to dislike his swimming lessons?

Hint and Answer on page 54

33. The Golf Ball

According to the PGA, the longest distance a golf ball ever traveled is 515 yards in 1974. Yet, one man made a large bet that he could hit a golf ball a mile. Keep in mind, a mile is 1,760 yards, more than three times the distance that a golf ball had ever traveled. He won the bet and hit the golf ball more than one mile.[4]

Question:
How did he do it?

Hint and Answer on page 55

34. Who Let the Horses Out?

Jeanne had five horses in her stable. At the end of the day, she put them in separate stalls, closing the bottom half of the stall door and latching it. Each morning, all five horses would be outside in the corral.[5]

Question:
How did this happen?

Hint and Answer on page 55

35. Marathon Runner

One man did a lot of traveling. He ran 50 marathons from September 17, 2006, through November 5, 2006. He is known as the 50/50/50 man.[6]

Question:
What does 50/50/50 represent?

Hint and Answer on page 55

36. Man in the Desert

A man was found dead in the desert lying on his back. He had with him the following items: a pack, a full water bottle, and a first aid kit.

Question:
How did he die?

Hint and Answer on page 56

37. Seahorses

Seahorses can give birth to many young ones, which can range from 5 to 1,000 or more newborn seahorses. However, there is something even more unusual about seahorses than birthing as many as 1,000 or more young ones.[7]

Question:
Can you guess what that might be?

Hint and Answer on page 56

38. Coins

I have in my pocket pennies, nickels, dimes, and quarters. I have at least two of each of these coins. My coins add up to less than two dollars.

Question:
Using this information, what is the maximum number of coins that I can have in my pocket while still remaining under two dollars?

Hint and Answer on page 56

39. What Did I Do?

They called me a hero, but I don't think of myself in that way. We did save 155 lives on that day. Since I was the captain, I seemed to get all the credit. But, I "remind everyone that this is about more than one person. It's about a crew."[8]

Question:
What did I do to be called a hero?

Hint and Answer on page 57

40. Burmese Python

I am a Burmese python, and I live with a man who thinks I am his pet. As I grew older, I picked up many skills living with him. Recently, I learned a new skill that would prevent us from being apart.[9]

Question:
What new skill did I learn?

Hint and Answer on page 57

41. Low on Fuel

While flying over the Atlantic Ocean, my large military plane was running out of fuel, and I did not have enough to get back to land. I did not want to ditch my aircraft, so I radioed for help. Eventually, I was able to land the plane at a coastal airbase.

Question:
How was this possible?

Hint and Answer on page 57

42. Surrounded

A man and his daughter Stephanie traveled to Yellowstone National Park. One morning while they were in their cabin, the man asked his daughter to go out to their car to get a flashlight. She went outside and immediately came back in because free-range animals had surrounded their car, which frightened her.

Question:
Which animals were surrounding their car?

Hint and Answer on page 58

43. One Surprised Alligator

An alligator thought he had bitten into a fine meal when he found this river creature. However, the alligator got more than he bargained for. Then, the creature swam safely away.[10]

Question:
Who was this river creature that surprised the alligator?

Hint and Answer on page 58

44. Conveyance

I carry a very important person, an American citizen born in the United States, to many destinations both nationally and internationally. I need to be in tip-top condition to do my job.

Question:
Who am I and what is my name?

Hint and Answer on page 58

45. A Lot in Common

A married couple has a daughter. Naturally, the three of them have a lot in common, but one thing stands out as truly remarkable. The odds of this occurrence happening in life is about 1 in 133,000.[11]

Question:
What is this remarkable occurrence?

Hint and Answer on page 59

46. What Word Am I?

I am a word that comes from history and has 10 letters. I begin with the letter "a" and end with the letter "m." Within me, there are at least three other words and one of them is "bell."

Question:
What word am I?

Hint and Answer on page 59

47. Home

In the past, I was a home for many people, but you would not necessarily say that about me today. Even if I offered you my protection, you might not accept my offer. However, if you did accept it, I suspect it would only be for a short time.

Question:
Who am I?

Hint and Answer on page 59

48. The Earth

The earth has a circumference of 24,901 miles. It makes one revolution in each 24-hour period, which means we are traveling over 1,000 miles per hour.

Question:
If we are traveling at over 1,000 miles per hour, why don't we feel it?

Hint and Answer on page 60

49. High Jump

Joe could regularly do a vertical jump of 20 inches, which wasn't bad for his age. His friend, Sam, once did a vertical jump of 120 inches or 10 feet, which was phenomenal.

Question:
Can you explain how this was possible?

Hint and Answer on page 60

50. Who Am I?

I was considered to be a military genius who won many battles and was blessed with a photographic memory. I once said, "A good sketch is better than a long speech." When playing cards, I often cheated.

Question:
Who am I?

Hint and Answer on page 60

51. Different Weights

A man living in Tennessee weighs 180 lbs. When he visits two other places in the world he has a different weight. In one place he weighs more, and in the other he weighs less.[12]

Question:
How is this possible? Where are the other two places?

Hint and Answer on page 61

52. Directions to Her New Home

Years ago before GPS, a woman was expecting four Christmas guests. She phoned them with precise directions, telling them where to turn left and where to turn right. She even told them to look in her front yard for a specific object, which would distinguish her home in the brand new cookie-cutter subdivision, since their street numbers had not been put up yet. But her guests still could not find her home.

Question:
Why did this happen?

Hint and Answer on page 61

53. You Won't Believe It

The longest golf ball drive occurred in 2004. You really will not believe this, but it has been estimated that the ball traveled approximately one million miles.[13]

Question:
How was this done?

Hint and Answer on page 61

54. My Lights

A woman just loved her fluorescent lighting in the laundry room, the garage, and the closets. They were bright and economical to use. At times, her garage lights just didn't seem to work right. It was as if they lost their brightness. At other times, they worked perfectly.

Question:
Can you explain why this happened?

Hint and Answer on page 62

55. Flying Times

A woman flies from Miami, Florida to Seattle, Washington on a nonstop flight with American Airlines. The trip is 2,722 miles and takes 6 hours and 27 minutes. On her return trip from Seattle to Miami on a nonstop flight with American Airlines, the trip is still 2,722 miles and takes 5 hours and 46 minutes.

Question:

Why does the return trip take less time than the original trip?

Hint and Answer on page 62

56. Keyless Car Remote

The normal range of a keyless car remote is usually between 20 and 60 feet. However, one man has found a way to increase this range to about 260 feet without using tools or external manmade devices.[14]

Question:
Can you tell me how he did it?

Hint and Answer on page 62

57. Upside Down Man

Gravity has its powerful effect on all of us. Believe it or not, one man has been able to run upside down briefly without falling.[15]

Question:
How he was able to do this?

Hint and Answer on page 63

58. Boat Dock

A man hired an electrician to run electricity underground from his log home to his boat dock, which was approximately 300 feet away. The electrician used a trench digging machine between the two locations. She laid the conduit, a plastic pipe, into the 300-foot trench and immediately covered it with dirt without running the electrical wire.

Question:
How did the electrician get the boat dock wired now that 300 feet of conduit has already been buried?

Hint and Answer on page 63

59. Breathing Ground

At first glance, a man thought it looked like the earth was breathing as he watched the ground around the trees moving in and out. He couldn't believe this was really happening.[16]

Question:
What accounted for this strange phenomenon?

Hint and Answer on page 63

60. Tipping Over

A man was concerned about tipping over in his canoe on the lake. He wondered how he could get back into the canoe if he did without tipping it over again. In the canoe he had 10 feet of rope, one paddle, one three-gallon bucket, and one dry bag suitable for dry and/or wet goods. When he tried to stand up, leaning too far to the right, the canoe tipped over.

Question:
How did he get back into the canoe?

Hint and Answer on page 64

61. Buried

People are buried in the United States in accordance with the regulations and policies of each state. Look at the question below.

Question:
Why can't a man living in Kentucky be buried west of the Mississippi River?

Hint and Answer on page 64

62. Roads and Highways

I have roads and highways, but I have no street lights. I have no fences or telephone poles, but I do have intersections.

Question:
Who am I?

Hint and Answer on page 64

63. Five-Letter Word

I am a five-letter word that has the same spelling whether you spell me forward or backwards. I begin with the letter "r."

Question:
What word am I?

Hint and Answer on page 65

64. Big Tunnel

There is a new tunnel running through the Swiss Alps designed for high-speed trains. It took 17 years to build at a cost of 9.3 billion euros. This tunnel is now the longest tunnel in the world, surpassing the Channel Tunnel between the United Kingdom and France, as well as others.[17]

Question:
If each mile took approximately 177.28 days to complete, how long is this new tunnel?

Hint and Answer on page 65

65. In Common

There are many interesting countries in this world of ours. Here are four countries that I have found to be fascinating: Ecuador, Columbia, Kenya, and Somalia.

Question:
What significant feature do these four countries have in common?

Hint and Answer on page 65

Chapter Three

ADVANCED PROBLEMS

66. Ping Pong

An amateur ping pong player challenged a professional ping pong player to a match, betting that he could beat him. The professional laughed at the prospect, but he took the bet anyway. The professional agreed to allow the amateur to choose the paddles. To his surprise, the professional lost.[18]

Question:
How did the amateur beat the professional player?

Hint and Answer on page 67

67. Survived

Though she was injured, a female flight attendant survived a fall from 33,000 feet without a parachute.[19]

Question:
Can you explain how this was possible?

Hint and Answer on page 67

68. Container

I am a large plastic container with a removable mesh liner. I can float in the ocean, but just barely. The top of my container is even with the level of the sea. A tube is attached to the bottom of my container and runs to a pump.[20]

Question:
What am I?

Hint and Answer on page 68

69. Top Secret Code

Here is another coded message, but it is more difficult than the previous one in this book.

Question:
Can you decode the hidden message below? <u>Write</u> down your answer and do not share it with anyone else.
24-19 / 12-5-26-9 / 5 / 10-22-13-9-18-8 / 29-19-25 / 17-25-23-24 / 10-13-22-23-24 / 6-9 / 5 / 10-22-13-9-18-8

Hint and Answer on page 68

70. Margie's Secret

Margie could write more words and letters in 30 minutes than any of her classmates. Even though she and her classmates wrote for the same amount of time, Margie wrote nearly double the amount of words than any of her classmates.[21]

Question:
How did Margie do it?

Hint and Answer on page 68

71. Tightrope Walking

A woman successfully walked across a slackline (tightrope). Interestingly, she started at one point and ended up more than a mile away, but her slackline was less than 200 feet in total length.[22]

Question:
How was this possible?

Hint and Answer on page 69

72. Is that an Oil Spill?

A photographer captured an image of an oil spill while flying in a small plane over the Atlantic Ocean. However, upon closer observation, it was determined that it was not an oil spill at all.[23]

Question:
Can you guess what it was?

Hint and Answer on page 69

73. Not as Popular Today

When you find me, I will always be outside. I will entertain you and others, but it will cost you. I am not as popular today as I was in the 1960s, but you can still find me if you are willing to drive around.

Question:
Who am I?

Hint and Answer on page 69

74. Moon Mission

The Apollo 13 moon mission incurred several problems during its journey. On its way to the moon, an explosion occurred and the crew was in jeopardy of not making it back to earth safely. They were more than 3/4 of the way to the moon when the explosion took place.[24]

Question:
Why didn't they turn back immediately and return to earth?

Hint and Answer on page 70

75. A Ten-Letter Word

I am a word that refers to the past not the present. I have ten letters, and I will tell you five of them. Three of them are the letter "e" and two of them are the letter "r." Additionally, there is one more pair of letters.

Question:
What word am I?

Hint and Answer on page 70

76. The Fishing Line

A man and his son went fishing. They had brand new 4 lb. line on their reels. At the end of the day, they loaded their boat onto the trailer and drove home in his 1963 Chevy truck. When they arrived thirty minutes later, one of their reels had no fishing line left on it.

Question:
Where was the fishing line? The man knew the answer, but his son did not.

Hint and Answer on page 70

77. The Landing

A man flew his small plane for an hour and then landed it. However, he did not touch the ground when he landed nor did he touch the dirt, the concrete, or the asphalt.[25]

Question:
Can you explain how this was possible?

Hint and Answer on page 71

78. Go West Young Man

People think I spout off, and I suppose they are correct. Because of my name they expect me to be on time, but sometimes I am late and sometimes I am early. However, it is usually not more than an hour or so in either direction. That's just the way I am. From Bar Harbor, Maine, go west young man, go west.

Question:
Who am I?

Hint and Answer on page 71

79. The Trampoline

A man jumped off a balcony that had no railing and landed on a trampoline below. Amazingly, he bounced back up to the exact same height as that of the balcony he jumped off of. This goes against the law of physics and doesn't seem possible.[26]

Question:
So, how did he do it?

Hint and Answer on page 71

80. Jellyfish

Swimming in the water when jellyfish are present is not a good idea. Jellyfish can deliver painful, stinging venom. However, one man went swimming with jellyfish and he wasn't harmed.[27]

Question:
How was this possible?

Hint and Answer on page 72

81. Needing a Charge

After her short shopping trip for her son's toy supplies, a woman found her car battery nearly dead. It had enough power to run the lights and windshield wipers, but not enough to start the engine.[28]

Question:
What did she do to start her car without getting help from anyone else?

Hint and Answer on page 72

82. Irrigation Shutdown

In the summer, a cattle farmer uses his irrigation system to water his apple orchard along the canal. His tractor is hooked up to an irrigation pump. It has a long perforated hose lying below the water level of the canal. When he started up the tractor everything was working fine, but when he returned a few hours later everything had shut down. So, he started up the tractor again and everything was working fine, but when he returned later it had happened again. Everything shut down. There was no evidence as to why this had happened.

Question:
Can you explain why the irrigation system kept shutting down?

Hint and Answer on page 73

83. Super Square

Look at the diagram below.

Question:
How many squares are in this figure? <u>Write</u> down your answer and do not share it with anyone else.

Hint and Answer on page 73

84. Pizza Delivery

Rob delivers pizza like no other pizza delivery person in the world. The pizza is delivered in a unique container. He uses a car for the first part of his delivery, but not for the second part, which requires that he wear specialized equipment. The chances are he will never deliver a pizza to you.[29]

Question:
Where is his pizza delivery destination?

Hint and Answer on page 74

85. Flying Saucers

In the 1960's, a man observed three silver discs above a wooded area in the night sky. They moved from left to right above the woods and then disappeared. The next night, he observed two silver discs above the woods move in the same way and then they disappeared. On the third night, he observed a single disc above the woods move across the night sky from left to right and then it disappeared.

Question:
Can you explain these phenomena?

Hint and Answer on page 74

86. McDonald's

A man drove to McDonald's every Sunday morning for breakfast. It was only two minutes from his mountain home. He would order scrambled eggs and sausage for two. Of the 52 weekly trips to McDonald's, about three times a year he would drive right past it and miss the turn.

Question:
Why did this happen to the man?

Hint and Answer on page 75

87. The Canoe

While working on his uncle's farm one summer, a boy built a lightweight canoe with limited materials. When it was finished he took his uncle on the maiden voyage. Their trip lasted only five minutes before the canoe sank in the middle of the canal, causing them to swim to shore.

Question:
Can you figure out why the canoe sank?

Hint and Answer on page 75

88. An Amazing Shot

A man has made an amazing basketball shot off a manmade structure in Switzerland. This was the highest basketball shot ever made, swishing through the net from a height of 583 feet. Furthermore, he made the shot in only three attempts.[30]

Question:
What structure did he shoot from to make this amazing shot?

Hint and Answer on page 75

89. Hula Hoop

One man twirled a hula hoop around his waist with the largest hoop anyone has ever tried. He managed to make it revolve around him six times before it fell to the ground. The average adult hula hoop has a diameter of 40 inches. The circumference of his hula hoop was 52.85 feet.[31]

Question:
Rounding to the nearest inch, how many inches is the diameter of his hula hoop?

Hint and Answer on page 76

90. Hoverboard

A boy rode a hoverboard inches above the pavement to the surprise of the crowd. It was amazing to watch, but could this be real? I think not.[32]

Question:
How did he do it?

Hint and Answer on page 76

91. Ice Cubes

A woman cut several ice cubes, one at a time, in half with a thin piece of graphite. It was not a knife, just a piece of graphite.[33]

Question:
How was this possible?

Hint and Answer on page 76

92. John's Gift

John has a special gift that only occurs in about one percent of the population. It has helped him in sports such as football, basketball, and baseball. Many athletes wish they had this gift.

Question:
Can you guess his special gift?

Hint and Answer on page 77

93. Two Ponds

A woman owned a Florida property with two clear freshwater ponds that were about 50 feet apart from each other. Pond A had fish in it, while pond B had <u>no</u> fish in it. One day she noticed fish in pond B.

Question:
How did this happen?

Hint and Answer on page 77

94. The Car

A man rented a car in Maui and went touring around the island. The car ran beautifully up the mountain to Haleakala National Park. After, enjoying the views, he got back in his car, but it would not start. He tried and tried, but he couldn't get it to work. Finally, a woman came by and fixed the problem immediately. She had seen this problem before.

Question:
What simple thing did she do to start the car?

Hint and Answer on page 77

95. Now You See Me, Now You Don't

You can see me at Christmas and sometimes at Easter, but the rest of the year I am on vacation. People do say I am pretty, and some say I am beautiful. I have been in many homes and maybe even in your home.

Question:
Who am I?

Hint and Answer on page 78

96. Overnight Lake

A man lives at the end of his street along a cul-de-sac, which is about 100 feet in diameter. In the fall after a hard rain, a small lake formed over the entire cul-de-sac, measuring as much as 12 inches deep in some places. He knew what to do, but it still took him an hour and a half to get rid of the overnight lake.

Question:
What was the cause of the lake? And what did he do to get rid of the overnight lake?

Hint and Answer on page 78

97. World Record

A man has set a new world record in the mile run. Oddly enough, he did not break the 4-minute mile mark although several other runners have. On the contrary, his record-breaking time was 5 minutes and 54 seconds.[34]

Question:
How could he be the current world record holder with a finish time of 5 minutes and 54 seconds?

Hint and Answer on page 79

98. Not a Fish

I am found in both freshwater and saltwater, but I am neither a fish nor any other type of living creature. I have been around for some time, perhaps from the beginning of time. You would say that I am no friend to small boats or canoes. I exist because of certain conditions.

Question:
What am I?

Hint and Answer on page 79

99. In the Trees

If you saw us in a tree you wouldn't believe it, but this is what we do. You can find us in a valley in Morocco. We like the fruit there.[35]

Question:
Who are we?

Hint and Answer on page 79

100. We Are Unique

We are lakes found in Mexico, and we are unique. Others of our kind do not look exactly like us. We may be similar in size and substance, but we have something beautiful that they do not.[36]

Question:
What quality do we have that makes us unique?

Hint and Answer on page 80

Chapter Four

BEGINNING PROBLEMS
HINTS AND ANSWERS

1. Tennis Tournament

Hint:
Each player loses once.

The Answer:
127 matches.

2. River Rocks

Hint:
What factors exist around a drainage ditch?

The Answer:
The landscape workers put a roll of felt under the river rocks, which allowed drainage from the heavy rainfall to lift up some of the river rocks and deposit them further down the drainage ditch.

3. Ant Survival

Hint:
Cooperation between the ants is the key to their success.

The Answer:
The ants build a bridge with their own bodies, and the bridge floats. Thus, the ants survive flooding.

4. Millie

Hint:
Wearing apparel.

The Answer:
Millie was wearing sunglasses, so no one noticed that she fell asleep.

5. The Tortoise

Hint:
He got some help.

The Answer:
Strangely, another tortoise helped him flip over.

6. The Bus Driver

Hint:
Remember, who is the driver?

The Answer:
The age of the person answering the question.

7. Two Coins

Hint:
Think about the wording of this problem.

The Answer:
One of the coins is not a nickel, but the other one is a nickel. The answer is a nickel and a 50-cent piece.

8. The Same Bass

Hint:
Look at the bass closely.

The Answer:
The hook from yesterday was still in his mouth.

9. Where to Build

Hint:
There is only one place on earth to build this house. Get your compass.

The Answer:
The North Pole.

10. How Many?

Hint:
Look again. The answer is within the problem.

The Answer:
None. Moses didn't build the ark. Noah did.

11. The Election

Hint:
It was a presidential election.

The Answer:
She did not win the Electoral College vote.

12. Finding Values

Hint:
O = 9

The Answer:
O = 9
X = 6
Y = 3

13. The Big Hawaiian

Hint:
Think about family.

The Answer:
The big Hawaiian was his mother.

14. The Elevator

Hint:
Something about the buttons.

The Answer:
She was a very short woman and could only reach as high as the 9th floor button.

15. Blue Hen Chicken

Hint:
I am a ferry ride away from New Jersey.

The Answer:
I am the state of Delaware.

16. You Know Me

Hint:
I have numbers.

The Answer:
A clock.

17. Christmas

Hint:
Where is the visitor?

The Answer:
It was Christmas in the southern hemisphere, where the seasons are the opposite of those in the northern hemisphere.

18. Spooky

Hint:
Things are not as they appear to be.

The Answer:
It was daylight.

19. Quicksand

Hint:
Think about where she was hiking.

The Answer:
High tide. The tide coming in could drown the woman.

20. Innocent

Hint:
Could seven eye witnesses be wrong?

The Answer:
He had an identical twin that he didn't know about who actually committed the bank robbery.

Chapter Five

INTERMEDIATE PROBLEMS
HINTS AND ANSWERS

21. The Paddle

Hint:
Look on the bank.

The Answer:
The man and his son threw rocks on the far side of the paddle, causing it to move slowly back to the shore.

22. Mary

Hint:
Mary is not who she appears to be.

The Answer:
Mary is a goldfish, and Tom is a cat. Tom knocked over the goldfish bowl, causing it to break, which left broken glass, water, and Mary dead on the floor.

23. Safe Crossing

Hint:

You may bring one back on the return trip across the river.

The Answer:

Take the chicken over first, and then go back and get the fox. Drop the fox off, but bring the chicken back. Drop the chicken off, and bring the feed over. Finally, go back and get the chicken.

There is another option, but the chicken is still first and the chicken feed is second.

24. Two Buckets

Hint:

Fill up the three-gallon bucket more than once.

The Answer:

Fill up the three-gallon bucket and pour it into the five-gallon bucket. Refill the three-gallon bucket. Take this water and fill the rest of the five-gallon bucket. Now, this leaves one gallon left in the three-gallon bucket.

Empty the five-gallon bucket. Next, pour the one-gallon left in the three-gallon bucket into the five-gallon bucket. Fill the three-gallon bucket again, and pour it into the five-gallon bucket. Now, you have four gallons.

25. Squares

Hint:
Look again to see <u>all</u> of the squares. Squares can <u>overlap</u> each other.

The Answer:
(1) Large 4x4 square + (16) single squares + (9) 2x2 squares + (4) 3x3 squares = 30 squares

26. Candy Limit

Hint:
You spell my name with five letters.

The Answer:
I am Idaho.

27. Line and Circles

Hint:
Draw the bottom half first.

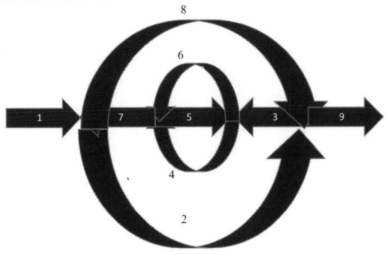

The Answer:
See the diagram above.

28. Four Things

Hint:
Think about how long the human body can go without food or water.

The Answer:
In the exact order:
1. Find or build a shelter. (Protect yourself from the elements.)
2. Find drinkable water. (Survive only three days without water.)
3. Build a fire. (Boil the water to make it safe to drink.)
4. Find food. (Survive three weeks without food.)

29. Still Standing

Hint:

This event happens in nature and thus, outdoors. It can be deadly.

The Answer:

Between 1942 and 1977, Roy Cleveland Sullivan was struck <u>seven</u> times by lightning and survived.

30. The Fall

Hint:

Sam is not who he appears to be.

The Answer:

Sam is an ant. His lack of mass allowed him to float on the air currents to the ground.

31. Coded Message

Hint:
Find the letter that corresponds to #1, and the rest will be easy to figure out.

The Answer:
To err is human
To forgive is divine.

32. The Pool

Hint:
What was it about this particular pool?

The Answer:
The pool was a salt-water pool, which was distasteful to the young boy and burned his eyes. Its water came directly from the Atlantic Ocean.

33. The Golf Ball

Hint:
Think about where he hit the golf ball.

The Answer:
He hit the golf ball on a frozen lake. The ball traveled a mile because the ice offered little to no resistance.

34. Who Let the Horses Out?

Hint:
Think about one's gifts.

The Answer:
One horse was able to use his mouth and lips to open the latch. He let himself and the other horses out.

35. Marathon Runner

Hint:
Count the days from beginning to end.

The Answer:
Dean Karnazes ran 50 marathons in 50 states in 50 days.

36. Man in the Desert

Hint:
One of his items explains his death.

The Answer:
He died because the pack with him was a parachute, and it did not open when he jumped out of the plane.

37. Seahorses

Hint:
Role reversal.

The Answer:
The male is the one who gives birth to the offspring, not the female.

38. Coins

Hint:
The key word is maximum.

The Answer:
125 coins: 119 pennies, 2 nickels, 2 dimes, and 2 quarters.

39. What Did I Do?

Hint:
Close to New York City.

The Answer:
Captain Sullenberger, known as "Sully," and his co-pilot successfully landed a plane in the Hudson River. On January 15, 2009, US Airways flight 1549 took off from LaGuardia Airport in New York City. After striking a flock of Canadian geese shortly after taking off, the engines failed. The emergency water landing was reportedly described by the National Transportation Safety Board as the most successful ditching in aviation history.

40. Burmese Python

Hint:
What can separate me from my owner?

The Answer:
I learned how to open a door.

41. Low on Fuel

Hint:
He had help.

The Answer:
I arranged a mid-air refueling, which allowed me to make it back.

42. Surrounded

Hint:
The animals were of the four-legged kind.

The Answer:
Bison were sitting around their car. According to the National Park Service, Yellowstone National Park has had bison living there since prehistoric times. It is home to the largest free-range herd of buffalos on public land in the United States.

43. One Surprised Alligator

Hint:
The creature had high energy.

The Answer:
An electric eel, which can generate both low and high voltage discharges.

44. Conveyance

Hint:
Not the first one.

The Answer:
The plane used for the Vice President. It is called Air Force Two.

45. A Lot in Common

Hint:
They celebrate together.

The Answer:
All three have the same birthday.

46. What Word Am I?

Hint:
Before.

The Answer:
Antebellum.

47. Home

Hint:
I am found in nature.

The Answer:
A cave.

48. The Earth

Hint:
Think about reference points.

The Answer:
Mountains, lakes, oceans, and the land are moving at this same constant speed with us. We have no fixed reference points to use while we are traveling, and the motion is constant.

49. High Jump

Hint:
Think about where this could happen.

The Answer:
His friend was an astronaut and did the jump on the moon.

50. Who Am I?

Hint:
I am European.

The Answer:
I am Napoleon Bonaparte.

51. Different Weights

Hint:
Consider the gravitational pull.

The Answer:
The gravitational pull is greater at the poles and less at the equator. In addition, centrifugal force is greater at the equator than at the poles. Thus, a person weighs slightly more at the poles and slightly less at the equator. One astronomer estimates that a person would weigh approximately 0.5% less at the equator than at the north or south poles.

52. Directions to Her New Home

Hint:
The season of the year.

The Answer:
The specific object was a snowman. Unfortunately, it melted between the time she gave her directions and the time her visitors were expected to arrive.

53. You Won't Believe It

Hint:
Think about where the person was when the golf ball was hit.

The Answer:
American astronaut Michael Lopez-Alegria hit a golf ball while he was tethered to the International Space Station in 2004. The ball was estimated to have traveled one million miles.

54. My Lights

Hint:
Think about the weather.

The Answer:
Her type of fluorescent lighting doesn't work as well when the temperature falls below the 40-50 degree range.

55. Flying Times

Hint:
Think about what could move the plane along faster when flying east.

The Answer:
The jet stream. When flying east, the jet stream provides a tailwind causing the plane to move faster. The exact opposite is true when flying to west. Another factor is the rotation of the earth, which benefits planes flying to the east.

56. Keyless Car Remote

Hint:
Think about the things you possess that would be available to enhance the range.

The Answer:
He put the remote to his chin. The electrical energy in his head helped to enhance the range of the remote.

57. Upside Down Man

Hints:

1. His run was extremely short with regard to both time and distance.

2. Think of a circle.

The Answer:
He ran inside a vertical wheel structure with a diameter of 10 feet. It only took several strides to complete the loop.

58. Boat Dock

Hint:
She used a common machine.

The Answer:
At one end of the conduit, she wadded up a piece of paper and tied it to a strong, lightweight string. At the other end, she hooked up a vacuum cleaner and turned it on. It sucked up the wadded paper tied to the string the entire 300 feet. She then attached the electrical wire to the string and pulled it through the pipe from the boat dock all the way to the house.

59. Breathing Ground

Hint:
The trees have shallow roots.

The Answer:
Intermittent gusts of wind blew against the trees with shallow roots, which made it appear as though the ground was breathing in and out.

60. Tipping Over

Hint:
Think about counter-balancing.

The Answer:
While treading water, the man flipped the canoe so that it was upright. He created a counter-balance by laying the paddle across the center of the canoe, tying it down to the middle thwart or crossbar. He filled the dry/wet bag with water and hung it at the end of the paddle, creating a good counter-balance. Then he swam around to the other side of the canoe and climbed in. Thus, he was able to get back into the canoe without tipping it over again.

61. Buried

Hint:
Look at the wording again.

The Answer:
You cannot bury a living man.

62. Roads and Highways

Hint:
I am for sale.

The Answer:
I am a map.

63. Five-Letter Word

Hint:
I was used during World War II, and I am still used today.

The Answer:
I am a radar.

64. Big Tunnel

Hint:
Solving the problem involves both multiplication and division.

The Answer:
The tunnel is 35 miles long.

65. In Common

Hint: Warm climate.

The Answer: The equator runs through all four countries.

Chapter Six

ADVANCED PROBLEMS
HINTS AND ANSWERS

66. Ping Pong

Hint:
The amateur player was allowed to select the paddles. He chose unique paddles.

The Answer:
He chose glass Coca-Cola bottles as the paddles to play in the game. He had practiced many days before the match using Coca-Cola bottles.

67. Survived

Hint:
She fell with part of the airplane.

The Answer:
Flight attendant Vesna Vuloric was pinned in by a serving cart in the tail section of the plane on January 26, 1972. The tail section broke off and fell hitting a snow laden hillside, which cushioned the impact. The snow slope slowed down the speed of the tail section.

68. Container

Hint:
I benefit our earth, and I do my best work when the ocean is calm.

The Answer:
I am an ocean garbage collector. Water flows over my top edge and down through the bottom tube and then pumped back into the ocean, while leaving the trash trapped in my removable mesh liner.

69. Top Secret Code

Hint:
Notice that 5 is the lowest number.

The Answer:
Assume the alphabet is numbered 1 through 26. So, this is letter +4 code which means "a" = 1 + 4 = 5. The letter "b" = 2 + 4 = 6, etc. The message is: To have a friend you must first be a friend.

70. Margie's Secret

Hint:
She has a special talent.

The Answer:
Margie is not only ambidextrous, but she can write with both hands at the <u>same time</u>.

71. Tightrope Walking

Hints:

1. Think about the two points.
2. Movement.

The Answer:
She walked across a slackline (tightrope) attached to two moving trucks traveling at 50 miles per hour. Faith Dickey performed this stunt on August 15, 2012 in Croatia.

72. Is that an Oil Spill?

Hint:
Something seems fishy to me.

The Answer:
It was a school of anchovies.

73. Not as Popular Today

Hint:
Think big.

The Answer:
I am a drive-in theater.

74. Moon Mission

Hint:
Physics can explain why they didn't turn around.

The Answer:
They used the moon's gravitational force to pull them around on a free trajectory back towards earth thus, saving precious fuel and energy.

75. A Ten-Letter Word

Hint:
The word begins with the letter "y."

The Answer:
I am the word "yesteryear."

76. The Fishing Line

Hint:
The truck.

The Answer:
The vehicle was an old 1963 Chevy truck, which had a small space between the bed of the truck and the truck body. The line came off the reel, fell into that space, and landed on the spinning driveshaft, which proceeded to pull off the entire 100 yards of fishing line.
Several days later when the man was putting things in the truck bed, he noticed the shiny line wrapped around the driveshaft.

77. The Landing

Hint:
He landed on something unusual, but familiar to you.

The Answer:
He landed on the top of a moving truck with a flat overhead surface.

78. Go West Young Man

Hint:
I have an endearing name.

The Answer:
Old Faithful. This geyser is located in Yellowstone National Park in Wyoming. It is a highly predictable geyser which has erupted every 44 to 125 minutes since the year 2000.

79. The Trampoline

Hint:
He did something that added to the jump.

The Answer:
He defied physics by pushing off the hard surface with his foot which gave extra momentum to the jump and increased the bounce off the trampoline.

80. Jellyfish

Hint:
No predators.

The Answer:
He swam in Jellyfish Lake. This stratified island lake had long ago had been cut off from the Pacific Ocean, except for three tidal tunnels, trapping the golden jellyfish population. Over time, the golden jellyfish lost most of their sting because they had been separated from any previous predators. Jellyfish Lake is located on Eil Malk Island, which is a part of the Rock Islands of Palau.

81. Needing a Charge

Hint:
She used what she had with her.

The Answer:
She had purchased 10 AA batteries, electrical tape, scissors, and insulated copper wire for her son on this shopping trip. Using her purchases, she hooked the batteries together to charge her car battery. After waiting awhile for it to charge, she was able to start her car.

82. Irrigation Shutdown

Hint:
Something is clogging the water intake hose.

The Answer:
Apples falling from the trees are being sucked onto the water intake hose, which shut down the pump. When the pump shuts down the apples from the hose are released and float to the top where they are eaten by the nearby cows leaving no evidence.

83. Super Square

Hint:
Some squares may overlap others.

The Answer:
55 Squares:
(1) Large 5x5 square + (25) 1x1 squares + (16) 2x2 squares + (9) 3x3 squares + (4) 4x4 squares

84. Pizza Delivery

Hint:
You have to be certified to use this special gear.

The Answer:
The destination is an underwater habitat in Key Largo, Florida. He wears scuba gear and carries the pizza in a watertight container to his hotel guest.

85. Flying Saucers

Hint:
In the sixties, stores having grand openings had a way of drawing attention.

The Answer:
In the sixties, store grand openings would draw attention to themselves by pointing searchlights into the night sky. The light shined through three cloud layers, producing three disc-shaped objects moving across the sky over the woods. On the second night, there were only two cloud layers. On the third night, there was only one cloud layer.

86. McDonald's

Hint:
A natural occurrence.

The Answer:
The fog was so heavy that he could not see the McDonald's.

87. The Canoe

Hint:
Think about different types of boat materials.

The Answer:
The boy had made the canoe out of canvas, which leaked badly and caused the canoe to sink.

88. An Amazing Shot

Hints:

1. What structure is that tall?
2. Water

The Answer:
A dam.

89. Hula Hoop

Hints:
1. Use the formula for circumference of a circle.
2. Circumference = 2 π r.
3. Use 3.14 for π.
4. Round to the nearest inch.

The Answer:
Diameter = 202 inches. The man's name is Yuya Yamada of Japan.

90. Hoverboard

Hint:
There must be something unseen to our eyes.

The Answer:
There was a magnetic track below the pavement that allowed the hoverboard to levitate.

91. Ice Cubes

Hint:
Think about transfer.

The Answer:
Heat from her hand transferred to the graphite piece which cuts through the ice cubes.

92. John's Gift

Hint:
A quarterback would love to have this gift.

The Answer:
He is ambidextrous, which allows him to use both hands equally well.

93. Two Ponds

Hint:
Some fish are better than others.

The Answer:
The fish were walking catfish (*Clarias batrachus*). Because they are air breathing and can prop themselves up on their fins and emulate a walking-like motion, the fish "walked" from pond A to pond B.

94. The Car

Hint:
Think about the higher elevation at the national park.

The Answer:
She removed the gas cap and then put it back on. This helped to equalize the pressure within the gas tank.

95. Now You See Me, Now You Don't

Hint:
I am not an animal, but I am alive.

The Answer:
I am a Christmas cactus (*Schlumbergera*). I regularly bloom at Christmas and sometimes at Easter depending on soil and light conditions.

96. Overnight Lake

Hint:
Consider the season of the year.

The Answer:
There was a metal grate drain at the end of the cul-de-sac. The grate was clogged with leaves, impeding the drainage. Once he removed the leaves, the lake began to disappear.

97. World Record

Hint:
A different kind of run.

The Answer:
Aaron Yoder runs backwards.

98. Not a Fish

Hint:
If a name were the hint, then mine would be Eddie.

The Answer:
I am a whirlpool.

99. In the Trees

Hint:
We are good climbers.

The Answer:
We are goats that can be found in the Argania trees in Tamri, Morocco, referred to as the "Tamri Goats." The fruit the tree produces attracts the goats who climb onto the branches to partake of the seasonal treat.

100. We are Unique

Hint:
Hue.

The Answer:
We are unique because we are pink lakes that were constructed by a salt company. The bright pink color is a result of the red colored algae, brine shrimp, and plankton living there.

REFERENCES

1 Wong, Caleb. "Turtle Rescuing its friend!" Online video clip. YouTube. YouTube, 4 Dec. 2014. Web. 12 Feb. 2018.

2 National Geographic. "Can You Survive Quicksand? I Didn't Know That." Online video clip. YouTube. YouTube, 19 Mar. 2013. Web. 15 Feb. 2018.

3 Wikipedia Contributors. "Roy Sullivan." Wikipedia, The Free Encyclopedia. Wikipedia, The Free Encyclopedia, Web. 12 Feb. 2018. http://wikipedia.org/wiki/Roy_Sullivan.

4 Grossman, Larry. "Amarillo Slim." Casino City Times. 1 June 2000. Web. 12 Feb. 2018. grossman,casinocitytimes.com/article/amarillo-slim-6391.

5 The Telegraph. "'Houdini' horse escapes from stable and frees friends." Online video clip. YouTube. YouTube, 20 Feb. 2013. Web. 12 Feb. 2018.

6 Televionet. "Dean Karnazes, the Ultramarathon Man, I run for 500 km but I am the average man." Online video clip. YouTube. YouTube, 13 Mar. 2012. Web. 15 Feb. 2018.

7 National Geographic. "Watch a Seahorse Give Birth to 2,000 Babies." Online video clip. YouTube. YouTube, 18 Mar. 2016. Web. 15 Feb. 2018.

8 Bennett, Mike. "Captain Sully Sullenberger and Jeff Skiles@Air Venture 2009 part 1 of 4." YouTube. YouTube, 8 Aug. 2009. Web. 23 April 2018.

9 Bermudaviper. "Giant Python opens doors." Online video clip. YouTube. YouTube, 19 June 2013. Web. 15 Feb. 2018.

10 RobsWTFRant. "Electric Eel Kills The Alligator - Must See The Alligator Dies." Online video clip. YouTube. YouTube, 13 Dec. 2010. Web. 15 Feb. 2018.

11 Inside Edition. "Mom, Dad and Newborn Baby All Share the Same Birthday." Online video clip. YouTube. YouTube, 17 Jan. 2017. Web. 15 Feb. 2018.

12 NIL. "Your Weight Varies at Different Places on Earth." Online video clip. YouTube. YouTube, 18 Dec. 2013. Web. 15 Feb. 2018.

13 Wein, Arron. "Who Hit the Longest Golf Drive Ever?" Web. 12 Feb. 2018. www.golflink.com.

14 Outrageous Acts of Science. "Using Your Head as a Transmitter." Online video clip. You Tube. YouTube, 20 Aug. 2015. Web. 15 Feb. 2018.

15 Pepsi Max. "Human Loop the Loop with Damien Walters." Online video clip. YouTube. YouTube, 19 Feb. 2014. Web. 15 Feb. 2018.

16 Afam Films. "The Earth Is ...Breathing. Trees 'Breathe' under a Forest Floor." Online video clip. YouTube. YouTube, 15 Nov. 2015. Web. 14 Feb. 2018.

17 Chan, Sewell. "World's Longest and Deepest Rail Tunnel, Through Swiss Alps, Opens." New York Times. 1 June 2016. Web. 15 Feb. 2018. http:///www.nytimes.com/2016/06/02/world/europe/goth ard-base-rail.

18 Grossman, Larry. "Amarillo Slim." Casino City Times. 1 June 2000. Web. 12 Feb. 2018. grossman,casinocitytimes.com/article/amarillo-slim-6391

19 The Iconic. "The Woman Who Survived 33,000 Feet Fall." Online video clip YouTube. YouTube, 26 Dec. 2016. Web. 15 Feb. 2018.

20 Tomo News US. "Ocean Cleaning Machine: Australian Surfers Quit Jobs, Invent Seabin to Clean Up Ocean." Online video clip. YouTube. YouTube, 5 Jan. 2016. Web. 16 Feb. 2018.

21 My London 1989. "Chinese Woman Who Can Write with BOTH Hands at the SAME TIME in Different Languages." Online video clip. YouTube. YouTube, 13 Dec. 2012. Web. 16 Feb. 2018.

22 CNN. "Woman Tightropes across 2 Speeding Trucks." Online video clip. YouTube. YouTube, 20 Aug. 2012. Web. 16 Feb. 2018.

23 STORYTRENDER by Caters TV. "Enormous School of Anchovies Looks Like Oil Slick." Online video clip. YouTube. YouTube, 24 July 2014. Web. 16 Feb. 2018.

24 "Apollo 13." Dir. Ron Howard. Imagine Entertainment, 1995. Film.

25 Gung Ho Vids. "Plane Lands On Moving Truck - Air Show Stunt." Online video clip. YouTube. YouTube, 24 Mar. 2016. Web. 16 Feb. 2018.

26 15 ft. Trampoline. "Extreme Trampoline Jumping." Online video clip. YouTube. YouTube, 18 Dec. 2013. Web. 14 April 2018.

27 ABC News. "Ginger Zee Travels to Palau's Jellyfish Lake." Online video clip. YouTube. YouTube, 11 May 2015. Web. 16 Feb. 2018.

28 ElectroBoom. "Jump Start a Car with AA Batteries." Online video clip. YouTube. YouTube, 19 June 2015. Web. 17 Feb. 2018.

29 Science Channel. "Scuba-Diving Pizza Delivery Man |World's Strangest." Online video clip. YouTube. YouTube, 19 June 2014. Web. 17 Feb. 2018.

30 How Ridiculous. "World's Record Basketball Shot 180m (593 Feet) |How Ridiculous." Online video clip. YouTube. YouTube, 20 Nov. 2016. Web. 17 Feb. 2018.

31 Guinness World Records. "Largest Hula Hoop Spun - Guinness World Records Day." Online video clip. YouTube. YouTube, 9 Nov. 2017. Web. 17 Feb. 2018

32 The Verge. "Riding the Lexus Hoverboard in Spain." Online video clip. YouTube. YouTube, 4 Aug. 2015. Web. 17 Feb. 2018.

33 Science Channel. "Slicing Ice with Your Fingers (and a Bit of Graphene)! |Outrageous Acts of Science." Online video clip. YouTube. YouTube, 23 May 2014. Web. 17 Feb. 2018.

34 Guinness World records. "Fastest Run Backwards One Mile - Guinness World Records." Online video clip. YouTube. YouTube, 31 Jan. 2016. Web. 17 Feb. 2018.

35 CBSN. "Tree-climbing Goats in Morocco's Argan Forest." Online video clip. YouTube. YouTube, 15 May 2016. Web. 17 Feb. 2018.

36 Expert Vagabond. "Las Coloradas Pink Lake - Mexico." Online video clip. YouTube. YouTube, 19 Oct. 2016. Web. 17 Feb. 2018.

ABOUT DAVE VACCARO

For more than thirty years, I served as a teacher and a principal. In my classroom, I presented kids with problems I already knew and those I had created. I always did this in a group setting so they could solve problems together. At home and on road trips, I presented many of these same problems to my own kids, to my nieces and nephews, and now to my grandkids. I live in Tennessee with my wonderful wife Leslie. For more problems and information, visit www.challengeyourkidsnow.com.

A CUSTOMER REVIEW

I hope you enjoyed using these problems and riddles with your kids. Please consider writing a short customer review. This would help us reach more teachers, more parents, and more kids. You can do this by going to amazon.com and search for *CHALLENGE YOUR KIDS* by Dave Vaccaro.

THANK YOU

Thank you for purchasing this book. I hope it helps you to challenge your kids in an enjoyable way. And as a way of saying thanks, I would like to offer you **five free problems and riddles** from my next book. Please email me at challengeyourkids@gmail.com, and I will send them to you.

Please share this book with your friends.

46573905R00057

Made in the USA
Middletown, DE
29 May 2019